suede

Edited by Chris Charlesworth.
Cover & book design by
Pearce Marchbank, Studio Twenty.
Computer management by
Adam Hay Editorial Design.
Picture research by David Brolan.

**Dedicated to
the memory of
Mick Ronson
(1946-1993)**

PHOTO: S.I.N. / M.GOODACRE

OMNIBUS PRESS

PHOTO: L.F.I. / TOM SHEEHAN

Exclusive Distributors:
Book Sales Limited,
8/9 Frith Street,
London W1V 5TZ, UK.
Music Sales Corporation,
225 Park Avenue South,
New York, NY 10003, USA.
Music Sales Pty Limited,
120 Rothschild Avenue,
Rosebery, NSW 2018, Australia.
To the Music Trade only:
Music Sales Limited,
8/9, Frith Street,
London W1V 5TZ, UK.

Printed by J.B. Offset Printers
(Marks Tey) Limited, Marks Tey, Essex.

A year is a long time in the pop world. Teen bands, dependent on the fickle loyalty of young fans, can come and go within a few months, leaving barely a trace of their existence. Likewise, a group that is in favour at the start of a year may find itself reviled as has-beens twelve months later.

Perhaps the best example of how fast things can move in the music business is the amazing rise of Suede, the Young Pretenders of 1993 who are sweeping all before them.

In April 1992 they were relative unknowns and had yet to release a record. Sure, they had fans but they were few in number. A year on, they achieved the seemingly impossible, shooting into the album charts at No 1 with their self-titled début album.

It sold more than 100,000 copies in its first week of release, outselling the number two LP, Depeche Mode's 'Songs Of Faith And Devotion', by a margin of at least two to one – with some claiming it was as high as four to one. Whatever the correct figure, Suede had truly arrived.

Even those with little more than a passing interest in the British pop world couldn't fail to notice this hot new band which had burst upon the scene, as if from nowhere, and made such an amazing impact. ▶

PHOTO: S.I.N / JOHN CHEVES

In the weeks prior to the release of Suede's LP it became almost impossible to open a magazine or paper without finding a picture of its charismatic singer, Brett Anderson. Wherever you looked – from gay magazines to national newspapers, fat colour supplements to breezy teen mags – there he was, his fringe flopped over his forehead, peering out of the pages.

As profiles, reviews and picture spreads piled up, the sceptics began muttering that the group were just hype – all glitz and no substance. And the fact that Suede's publicists won an award for promoting them lent further credence to these claims.

But the sceptics would do well to remember the old adage: there's no smoke without fire. A band rarely attracts the media's attention unless there is reason to spark such interest.

Admittedly, recent pop history is littered with examples of groups who were hailed by the music press as the next big thing – only to become last year's thing in record quick time. But a group that is championed by the press will soon be rumbled unless it comes up with the goods.

What's different about Suede is that they've proved they're special, first with the critics and now with the fans. For once, the hype seems to be justified. ▶

The story begins in the sleepy Sussex town of Haywards Heath. Twelve miles from Brighton, it has a population of just 22,000, most of whom enjoy a comfortable middle class life-style. Not a lot goes on. Even the Town Clerk admits: "It's probably most famous for its railway line." That tells you all you need to know about the place. In future, though, residents will be able to say it's the home of Suede.

Brett was born on September 29, 1967, on a local council estate. His family had little money but led a bohemian existence. His mother, now dead, was an unsuccessful artist but he credits her for his creative side. His father, Peter, trained as a chef but spent much of Brett's childhood out of work.

In interviews, Brett has described his father as "a mad old Englishman". And he certainly sounds eccentric. He wore his tie in the bath and every year visited the birthplace of classical musician Franz Liszt in Hungary, where he would kiss the ground and bring back soil as a souvenir.

"His three heroes are Liszt, Nelson and Churchill," Brett told *Q* Magazine. "And on their birthdays he puts a Union Jack outside his house on a flagpole. It used to bug the shit out of me when I was a kid but now I think it's one of the greatest things ever." Today, his father scrapes a living as a minicab driver and basks in the reflected glory of his son's fame. ▶

As a child, Brett claims he was timid and frightened of almost everything. And despite growing up in a seemingly model town, he nurtures a lasting hatred for Haywards Heath. "It was a horrific little place," he says. "It was much tougher than almost anywhere in London. When I was growing up there I was always aware of the vivid undercurrent of violence."

He met bassist Mat Osman, also born in 1967, and the product of a one-parent family with a similarly deprived background, at the local Oathall school and the two struck up a close friendship. They went on to form a band together at sixth form college called Geoff, playing gigs at the Town Hall. (They told one magazine they played in a band called Suave and Elegant. It was a joke!)

At school, Brett, who was "clever and hardworking" according to a friend, soon stood out from the crowd. The first time Mat met him he was wearing a pink suit. By the age of 16, he was sporting a tuxedo and then took to wearing a yellow suit around town in an attempt to ape David Bowie's 'Let's Dance' look. He even dyed his hair blond to perfect the image.

He acquired his Bowie fixation after listening to his big sister's record collection, following an early love for punk groups like Crass and Discharge. But trying to look like his hero made him an easy target for Haywards Heath's small town yobs with their even smaller minds.

"It started when I was about nine or ten and just carried on. They called me a queer and I was always getting beaten up. I couldn't wait to leave." ▶

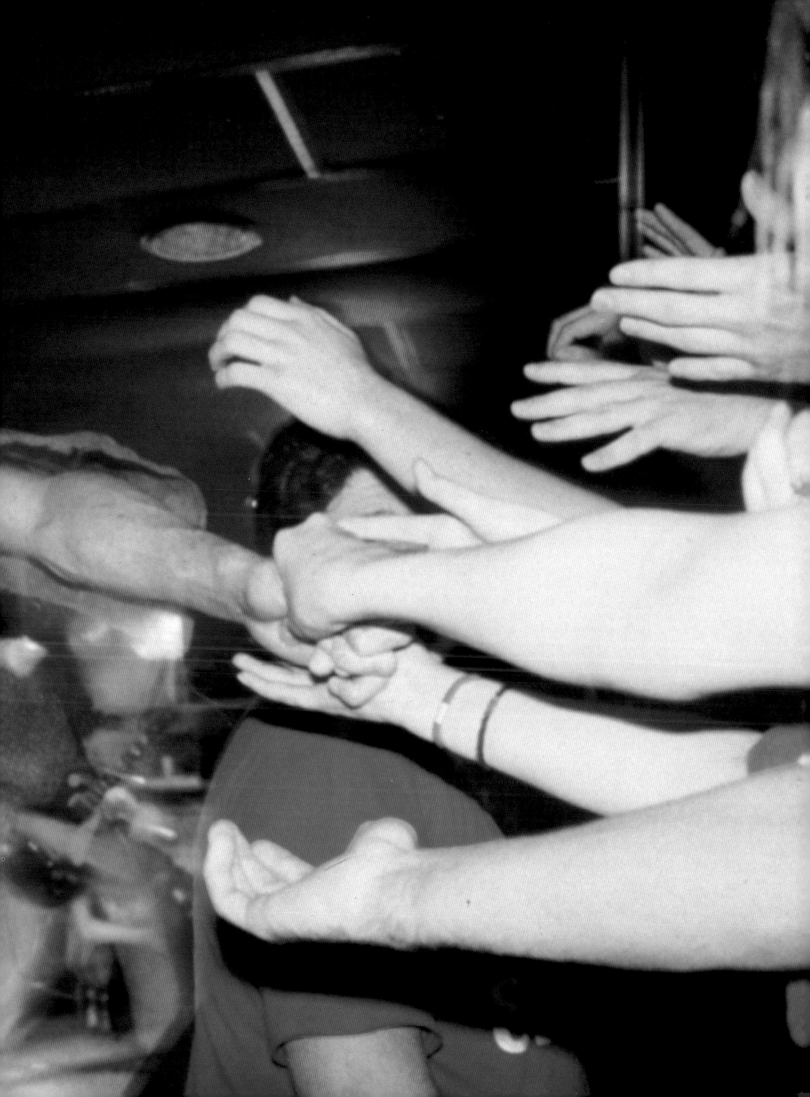

For years, Brett, who claims that growing up in Haywards Heath excluded him "from anything remotely interesting", dreamed of escape, a recurrent theme in Suede songs. He wanted to go somewhere glamorous and exciting where he could dress as he pleased without being victimised. The place was London. And it would soon become his adopted home.

He moved there when he was 19 to study Town and Country Planning at University College, London, but almost immediately switched subjects after falling in love with a beautiful architecture student, Justine Frischmann, who would play a key role in Suede's early days. Meanwhile, his old friend, Mat, had enrolled at the London School of Economics.

After the years of longing, Brett was ecstatic to find himself in the capital. "I've always loved London," he told *Melody Maker*. "I've always had a romantic vision of it. Even when I was small and my parents used to take me on day trips I got a shiver of excitement just arriving at Victoria. I always felt that was where I belonged."

Despite moving into a "shithouse" in Finsbury Park, The Smoke – with its dirt, grime and rubbish-strewn streets – lost none of its allure for the newcomer. "I went through a period of just walking around London on my own, just lapping everything up," recalls Brett. "I loved this huge, steaming mass of people."

His open-eyed awe for the sights and sounds of the city echo the reaction of another poor boy from a small southern town on visiting London some fifteen years earlier ...one Paul Weller. ▶

Despite coming to London supposedly to study and further their career prospects, Brett and Mat always had one eye on music, and they advertised for a guitarist in the *New Musical Express* in October 1989. The first person to respond was Bernard Butler, born on May 3, 1970.

The Haywards Heath lads were impressed, to say the least. "He just fitted in straight away," says Mat. "You virtually know within 15 seconds when someone's right." Looks were important, too. The new guitarist had to fit in with their idea of the group's image. Bernard, with his lanky frame and long dark hair, was perfect.

And the nascent band, which now consisted of Brett, his girlfriend, Justine, and Bernard on guitars, and Mat on bass, spent the next few months in Brett's bedroom to the accompaniment of a drum machine, writing songs and rehearsing. With hindsight Brett admits, not surprisingly, that the band were "unripe, musically" at this time.

By early 1990, though, they had enough songs to play a set and agreed it was time to make their live début. But first they had to find a name. There were various suggestions. Mat liked The Southern Way while Bernard fancied I Pray. But thankfully for all concerned, they plumped for a name put forward by Justine – Suede. ▶

"Everyone liked the idea," reveals a friend, "because there was the 'Suedehead' connection with Morrissey and the Blue Suede Shoes rock'n'roll link. It was visually good, too." This theme is taken up by Brett : "It's important to avoid clumsiness. Short names always look better on posters. And we loved the way the "s" and the "u" are together in Suede. It's an unusual-looking word."

With a name decided, they were ready to take to the stage – and played their first-ever gig at The White Horse in West Hampstead on March 10, 1990, supporting The Prudes and The Ruby Tuesdays. Brett claims it was the most exciting night of his life. Says a friend: "About 20 people were there for Suede, mostly friends of the band, and Bernard broke a string. The highlights were a couple of early songs, 'Justice' and 'Natural Born Servant'."

But any illusions the band had that stardom was just around the corner were rudely shattered in the months ahead when they couldn't even get gigs. In an interview, Brett revealed: "Getting started up was incredibly difficult, and for a time, we'd take any old crap. Only a few people were interested but they were so important. Without them we couldn't have even got on the first rung."

In a bid to get more live dates, Suede booked into a £35-a-day, eight-track studio to record a demo. A pirate station in London's East End played a couple of the songs, helping them land more gigs. A few weeks later, they got together £200, went into a 24-track studio and recorded a song which found its way onto the BBC's London radio station, GLR. As a result, they got a gig at London's Powerhaus. ▶

Meanwhile, Brett had moved into a seedy one-bedroom flat in London's trendy Notting Hill – home to, among others, former Clash frontman Joe Strummer. The group had also advertised for a drummer in the music press and even auditioned ex-Smiths star Mike Joyce. In the end they recruited Simon Gilbert after bumping into him at a gig. A former punk, Simon hailed from another sleepy country town, Stratford-Upon-Avon.

Then it seemed as if Suede landed their big break. A friend of a friend was setting up a record label in Brighton, liked their demo and said he wanted to sign them and record two songs for a single, provided the band signed a deal. Two tracks were duly recorded, 'Be My God' with Mike Joyce on drums and 'Art' with newcomer Simon Gilbert. Justine played guitar on both tracks. The single never materialised, apart from 50 white label copies which are now expensive collectors' items though now, surprise, surprise, there are plans to release the song – and the matter is in the hands of lawyers.

Frustrated by the group's lack of success, Justine left to resume her studies. And now that Brett had gained a degree in Architecture, crunch time had come. Would he and the others put away their instruments, pursue sensible careers and look upon Suede in years to come as a bit of youthful fun? Or would they risk all in a bid for pop stardom? ▶

Of course, there was no real choice. Could you see Brett poring over architects' drawings in a dreary council office? Hell, no. This was someone who claims he'd known since his schooldays that he was going to make it in the music business. Says Brett: "Even then I had the idea of the band I was going to be in. I was just waiting for it to happen."

However, the next 18 months were to test even Brett's astonishing faith in himself. With no regular income, the band had to get by on next to nothing. Even allowing for the hyperbole, it's clear there must have been moments when they all wondered whether it was worth the effort.

"We lived in emotional squalor for a year-and-a-half," says Mat. "We were despised by everyone. It was typical for Brett to borrow a quid in the morning: 50p for his dinner and 50p for the cat's." But of necessity they had to buy second-hand, crimplene clothes which have since become their trademark. Says Brett: "Things were desperate for ages."

Playing gigs at the Amersham Arms and other dives did little for their confidence. Their look and sound, which drew inspiration from 1970s Glam Rock, was seriously out of step with the times. Audiences responded either with catcalls or complete silence. Brett's camp stage manner came in for particular flak. Recalls Bernard: "Once we supported Teenage Fanclub and people just stood there saying nothing after we'd played, looking at us, almost disgusted." ▶

PHOTO: S.I.N. / IAN T. TILTON

PHOTO: CORA O'KEEF

But ironically the repeated setbacks made Suede what they are today: one of the most exciting new bands in Britain. All too many groups would have thrown in the towel at this stage. However, the outside world's hostility cemented the band's sense of identity and forced Suede's song writing axis of Brett and Bernard to go back to basics and learn how to write a truly great song.

"The key point was when things weren't happening on a business level," Brett told *Melody Maker*, "and we had a lot of time on our hands. So we spent ages learning how to write, just sitting around and thinking about songs. We picked out classic songs by The Beatles and Bowie, worked out how they were done and tried to play them note for note, thinking about why they were so good."

Slowly, but surely, their persistence paid off. There was no instant change of luck – that was yet to come – but they began to sense the improvement. Their live performances grew in confidence and Brett was perfecting the mannerisms (the pouting and eyelid fluttering, the wiggling of his bum and a cockney drawl *à la* Bowie) that would help get the band noticed.

Most crucially, they had complete confidence in their new material. Says Bernard: "We wrote 'The Drowners' and this batch of songs that we thought were just great and we became convinced that, even if it was the last thing we ever did, people would get to hear these songs." ▶

A buzz was beginning to grow about the band. A gig at the Powerhaus attracted a rave review in *Melody Maker* and their show at The Camden Falcon in February, 1992, attracted a sell-out crowd (still only 150 people), including Suggs of Madness and one of the group's heroes, former Smiths' front-man Morrissey.

Independent record companies showed interest in signing them but after their earlier experience, Suede were reluctant to sign a long-term deal. They also, perhaps somewhat arrogantly, saw themselves as too big a band to stick with a tiny label for long. As Brett explains: "We were being asked to sign eight-LP deals which was out of the question. If you're any good you can't even consider being on an indie label in ten years' time."

But one new label, Nude, set up by former A&R man Saul Galperno, who'd been instrumental in signing Simply Red to Elektra, offered the group just what they wanted: a two-single deal. They signed. Galperno had no doubt Suede were destined for big things, describing Brett as a "a born prima donna, a true star".

However, before the band could put out their first single something happened that was to dramatically change their fortunes. On April 25, 1992, their faces were plastered over the front page of *Melody Maker* alongside a headline proclaiming them the best new band in Britain. Never before had a group yet to release a record received such wild acclaim. ▶

PHOTO: L.F.I. / KEVIN CUMMINS

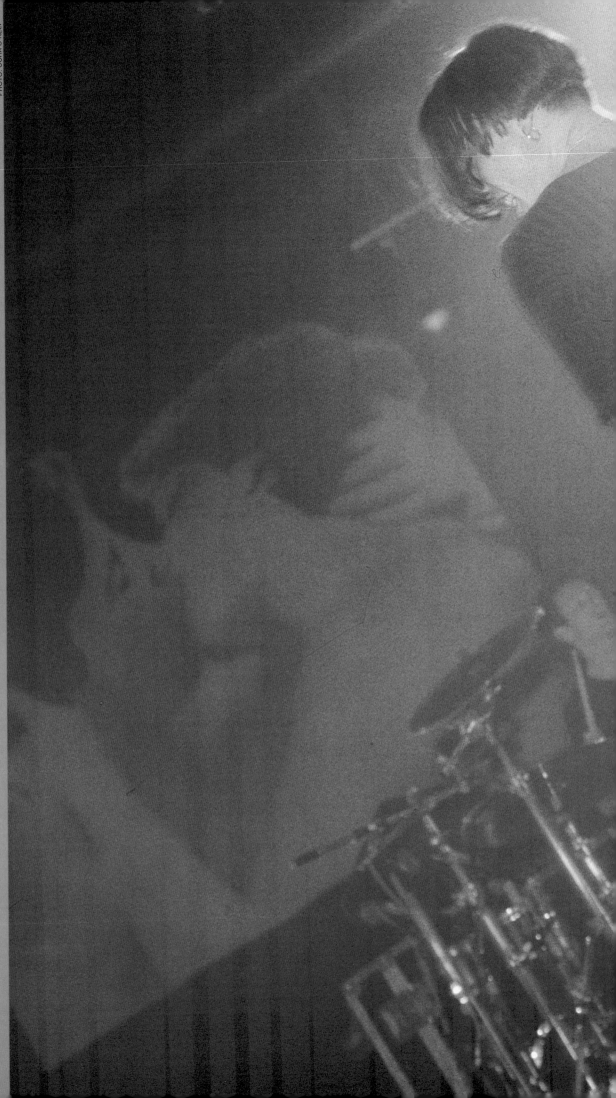

Inside a feature on them began with Brett saying "My fantasy has always been to have a song about a bizarre sexual experience in the Top Ten." Later in the piece, Bernard explained that the reason their music was twisted and sexual was because they were "English, twisted and sexual."

Right from the start, Suede set themselves apart from other rising stars in the indie world, establishing the themes they have pursued ever since: sex, drugs, despair, obsession, suicide and escape. Some of their lyrics would also have homo-erotic overtones. Not for them the jangly, happy songs of a thousand faceless indie bands.

The *MM* article was gushing in its praise, talking of Suede as a pop phenomenon and claiming they were the only band on the planet that actually mattered. One thing was for sure, it could not have given them a better launch pad for the release of their first single a couple of weeks later.

The Drowners opened with a driving riff and an infuriatingly catchy chorus – and was deservedly voted single of the week in both the *New Musical Express* and *Melody Maker*. The song, described by Brett as "about two people drugged up on sex in an obsessional relationship", topped the indie charts and reached No 49 nationally.

Both tracks on the flip side – 'My Insatiable One', an even more risqué song, containing a reference to male blow-up dolls, and 'To The Birds', a live favourite – were also memorable, giving substance to Suede's out-rageous claim that they were unable to write B-sides. ▶

Its intriguing cover, with a picture of a female model made up to look like a man, with her naked body hidden beneath a painted-on outfit, was another pointer to the band's gender contradictions and interest in gay imagery. A similarly styled, and equally striking, picture of Brett photographed with a blue shirt painted directly on to his skin, would appear on the front cover of *NME* in early 1993. The idea, however, seemed a rather blatant tip of the hat towards actress Demi Moore's controversial front cover pose (with a man's suit painted over her nude body) for *Vanity Fair* in 1991.

With the group having proved that they could, indeed, come up with the goods, interest in them blossomed. They supported indie band Kingmaker on tour and several reviewers preferred Suede to the headline act. They also put in an appearance at the Reading Festival. Their gigs soon became events, with scenes of growing hysteria. Brett's shirt was ripped off twice at London's 100 Club, and the record giants began sniffing around.

A six-track demo recorded by Suede was doing the rounds, and whereas a year before no-one wanted to know, this time labels were falling over themselves in a bid to sign up the band of the hour...but "the chase" had its amusing moments. One poor A&R man dashed around Scotland trying to sell Suede T-shirts in a bid to ingratiate himself with the group but was to be bitterly disappointed. ▶

Meanwhile, Suede were making the most of their new-found fame. They recorded a version of The Pretenders' 'Brass In Pocket' for *NME* compilation album, 'Ruby Trax', and the group's singer, Chrissie Hynde, revealed she preferred it to the original. Praise indeed!

Over the next few months, a series of interviews helped raise Suede's public profile even further. And the fact that Brett always gave "good copy" resulted in them getting more and more column inches in the press – be it *NME* or *The Independent*. Saul Galperno's claim that Brett had star quality was amply borne out.

Whatever the topic, whatever the question, Brett had something to say. Whether it was the Monarchy, "stupid, ugly people"…Grunge, "I am sick of it, it's a mask for people with no talent"… Madonna "so overrated and unsexual"… or Suede, "I'm a ridiculous fan of the band"… he always had an opinion.

And he revealed more about his own musical tastes when he made The Smiths' 'This Charming Man' his single of the decade while reviewing the latest releases for *NME*. "It's a truly magical song," said Brett, also telling how Morrissey was a fan of the band and was singing a Suede composition – 'My Insatiable One' – on tour. (The mutual admiration was not to last, though.)

But Brett became best known for talking provocatively about the ambiguous nature of his own sexuality and its bearing on his songs. For example, "I just don't feel I'm a fully-fledged member of the male sex." And echoing Morrissey on another occasion, he said: "I'm quite interested in lying back and taking it. And that's traditionally a female thing, isn't it?" ▶

Again, in a statement guaranteed to raise eyebrows, he told *Melody Maker*: "I see myself as a bisexual man who's never had a homosexual experience." The claim exposed him to the charge that he was simply adopting a quasi-gay pose in order to lend himself a certain aura, something he vigorously denied, arguing: "The only validation I need for what I do is that sometimes I feel like a woman."

Perhaps most controversially, though, he appeared to defend bestiality, claiming: "Most music treats sex as something very straightforward whereas in lots of cases it's completely deviant. Love is love, in whatever form it takes, whether between a man and an object, or an animal or another man." What would the RSPCA say?!

In September, Suede released their second single, 'Metal Mickey', which was duly voted single of the week in *NME* and *Melody Maker*. It went straight into the charts at No 17, and as a result, the band appeared on *Top Of The Pops* – a dream come true for Brett who had been an avid viewer of the show since childhood.

The presenter was understandably perplexed by the sight of Brett beating his backside with his hand and commented on his "interesting use of a mike stand". Whatever the response, no-one could deny that here, at last, were a group who dared to be different. ▶

PHOTO: S.I.N. / IAN T. TILTON

"I wrote 'Metal Mickey' in my head on the Tube," Bernard told *Guitar* magazine. "It was actually inspired by 'The Shoop, Shoop Song'. I love that stomping Sixties beat and I think it's a really sweet song so I put it together with this big chugging guitar part." Explaining how the band wrote songs, he continued: "I normally demo things with Simon in the studio, then Brett takes it away to write the lyrics and then we'll rearrange it again. I work out the guitar melodies as if I'm singing them."

The Anderson/Butler song writing partnership had now been picked up on by the music press which was soon drawing analogies with other great singer/guitarist writing teams – like Mick Jagger/Keith Richard and Morrissey/Johnny Marr – of the past.

Interestingly, both cite similar musical influences. Asked to select 12 songs that changed his life, Brett chose, among others, David Bowie's 'Bewlay Brothers', Iggy Pop's 'Lust For Life' and The Jam's 'Going Underground'. While Bernard, who took up the guitar when he was thirteen, listed Blondie, The Jam and The Specials.

By now, the band were keen to play down the "glam rock" tag that was beginning to dog them, and distance themselves from other so-called "glam bands" like Sweet Jesus, Denim and Verve. The influence of Bowie – and other Seventies stars like Mott The Hoople and Steve Harley – was obvious to anyone who liked Suede but was perhaps being over-emphasised. ▶

"I don't think we sound Glam" says Bernard. "Sometimes I do use similar sounds but they're great sounds and I'm into exploring good guitar sounds. I never listened to Bowie until about two years ago and the only thing I knew of his was 'Space Oddity' and 'Let's Dance'. The Glam thing's really pissed me off but we can ride it out."

Glam band or not, the record company bosses had their fat chequebooks out and were talking silly money. One American giant, Geffen, (whose roster of artists includes Nirvana, Guns N'Roses and Sonic Youth), flew Suede out to LA and reportedly made them a £6 million offer – a million quid an album.

It must have been tempting but the band eventually signed with Sony for a figure said to be in excess of £1 million. It was agreed their British records would still be released on Nude but benefit from Sony's corporate muscle. Elsewhere in the world, Sony would have a clean sweep. The band seemed to have got the best of both worlds.

Meanwhile, Suede made a triumphant return to the White Horse (the scene of their live début), playing a secret gig billed as a Nude Night Special, and were the subject of stories in several national newspapers – including The *Times*, *Observer* and *Daily Mirror*. However, it wasn't all fun and games. They had to start work on their album. ▶

The year couldn't have come to a better end for the band. Their seven-inch début, The Drowners, was voted single of the year by *NME* and *Melody Maker*. 'Metal Mickey' also finished in both papers' Top Ten. While the readers' poll results in the music press showed the public were as excited about Suede as the critics.

Pundits hailed 1992 as the year when a group had finally emerged with the power, vision and song writing skills to take on the world and reassert the rightful supremacy of British rock. And the same people predicted that Suede would be even bigger in 1993.

Work was proceeding well on the band's début LP, which was being produced by Ed Buller (who had worked with them on their first two singles). And in February, they released their third single, 'Animal Nitrate', a hard-edged song that looked sure to be a hit.

Although the band played the song at the BRITS Award, they failed – scandalously, some felt – to win a nomination in the best new artist category. But the music press yet again gave a Suede disc the thumbs up. Both *NME* and *Melody Maker* voted 'Animal Nitrate' single of the week, and it duly crashed into the Top Ten. On the flipside was another live favourite, 'Painted People', and a ballad about the perils of fame, 'The Big Time'.

The single finally made Suede a household name, but it was to be their most controversial hit to date. The ambiguity of the lyrics lent themselves to various interpretations. Many critics thought the song was about gay sex and the title itself a word play on amyl nitrate, a favoured drug in gay clubs. ▶

On the eve of its release, Brett raised the stakes even higher by openly talking about his drug use. He told *NME* "The idea for the song came in a period when drugs were replacing people in my life. Sex was just a hollow, vacuous thing and I was doing lots of coke and Ecstasy."

And he went on to virtually admit that rumours about his prodigious drug use in the studio were true, saying "I'm quite obsessed by drugs. I've always seen drugs as quite useful to song writing – and song writing is the most important thing in my life."

Whatever the truth of the matter, he shouldn't have been surprised when a tabloid followed up his comments by splashing the story of Suede's "drug shame" in big, bold letters on its pop page. Of course, they say all publicity is good publicity – but getting close to drugs can be costly. Ask Boy George.

The video for the song also sparked controversy because it showed two men kissing and was duly banned from ITV's *Chart Show*, despite the band's protests.

Interestingly, despite Suede's, and in particular Brett's, flirtation with homo-erotic themes, the only member of the band who is gay is drummer Simon Gilbert. He says "Fans instantly assume that I'm straight because I haven't got long hair." Playing down the band's homosexual over-tones, though, he adds "It doesn't matter whether Brett's gay or not – he sings universally.". ▶

With the single riding high in the pop charts, Suede went on a short tour. By now, their gigs were selling out instantly and they had acquired a hard core of fans who followed them all over the country – the so-called Suedettes. Crazed female fans would regularly tear off Brett's shirt during shows. One loyal follower moaned "He's lost so many beautiful clothes."

In April their long-awaited début album, simply called 'Suede', was released. It took three months to make and was recorded, at a cost of £105,000, at Master Rock Studios in Kilburn, London. Some of the reviews betrayed a slight sense of disappointment but that was more of a reflection on the critics than the band. The music press, not for the first time, had worked themselves into such a frenzy that they had forgotten that Suede were only human.

It was a fine début, though. Prior to its release, Brett had said he would not be satisfied if it contained one duff track. He needn't have worried, every song worked. Those people only familiar with the singles may have been surprised by the number of slower tracks. But, if anything, this helped make it more of a rounded album.

The cover, which showed two women locked in a passionate clinch, sparked a bit of healthy controversy and the *Daily Mirror* reported a family watchdog's concern over the picture. Few fans were offended though, and the album rocketed to No 1, proving that Suede were now arguably the biggest, as well as the best, new band in Britain. ▶

Initially only 150,000 copies of the record, which included all three singles, were pressed. But demand was so great that a second pressing was ordered within two weeks. However, the band's hour of glory was tarnished by what's been dubbed Suedegate. It began with an article in *The Face* magazine revealing Brett's views on meeting Morrissey. He was quoted as saying "I didn't particularly like Morrissey. He's so ridiculously shy, it's boring, not charming. He's like some kind of useless teenager."

A few weeks later, Morrissey hit back in the war of words accusing Suede of lacking originality and telling *Vox* magazine "Despite his claims to the contrary, I have never met Brett and wouldn't wish to; he seems like a deeply boring young man." On hearing of the rebuke, Brett was visibly shocked and claimed *The Face* had misconstrued his comments.

By now, the press were talking about "a feud" between the two stars. A third party, *The Face*, joined in the row, standing by its story and announcing that it had Brett's comments on tape. Whoever you care to believe, the incident was a timely reminder of how a flippant comment made by someone in the public eye could be blown out of all proportion. However, the controversy is unlikely to do either party any harm.

Our story more or less ends, for the time being, at least, with the cancellation of a headlining gig at the Kilburn National just days after Suede's album had gone to No 1. Police chiefs feared a riot after 1,000 too many tickets were sold and they pulled the plug. It was yet another sign of the snowballing hysteria surrounding the band. ▶

In a bid to soothe upset fans, Suede announced they would be giving away a free flexi-disc, featuring an acoustic version of 'My Insatiable One', at two new gigs at the Brixton Academy in mid-May, timed to coincide with the release of their fourth single 'So Young', one of the best tracks on their album.

What of the future? Will Suede repeat their success worldwide? They certainly have the looks, charisma and talent. But a lot of great British groups (just think of The Jam and Madness) never made it in the States. Even if they don't, does it matter? Suede are a peculiarly English band and happily admit they have little interest in America.

Of course, the press likes nothing better than to build up a band and then knock 'em down. But Brett believes they can survive the hype, saying "People forget that to get anywhere you have to be good."

Just as important, Suede are still hungry. Like so many British bands, they are a product of the class system. As one friend says "If I'd grown up like Brett, with bugger all, surrounded by people who were stinking rich, I'd have something to prove." Forget the sceptics, Suede will be around for a long time yet.

PHOTO: L.F.I. / TOM SHEEHAN